bio.

hello,

I am Sabrina Smith.

AUTHOR. FINANCIAL EXPERT. LIFE COACH AND ELDER

I0617197

I have gained much wisdom and understanding as one called to be Gods' Intercessor. I have experienced attacks and challenges in my life, especially in the area of finances. God helped me to overcome financial challenges by using the principles of the word of God.

This freedom has given me the insight and revelation to help other Intercessors access their wealthy place and gain the freedom needed to be victorious in every area of their life. As a skilled mentor, I will coach you through the strategies needed to access your wealthy place. Don't worry you are in good hands.

I've lead Prayer Teams, Prayer Conferences, Trained and Mentored Intercessors.

This Financial Planner will unlock strategies that you'll need to meet your financial goals and overcome the challenges of not having enough. It is Gods' will that you and I occupy the wealthy place.

SIGNED,

~Sabrina Smith,

IT'S TIME TO INCREASE

PROVERBS 3:9-10

Copyright Page

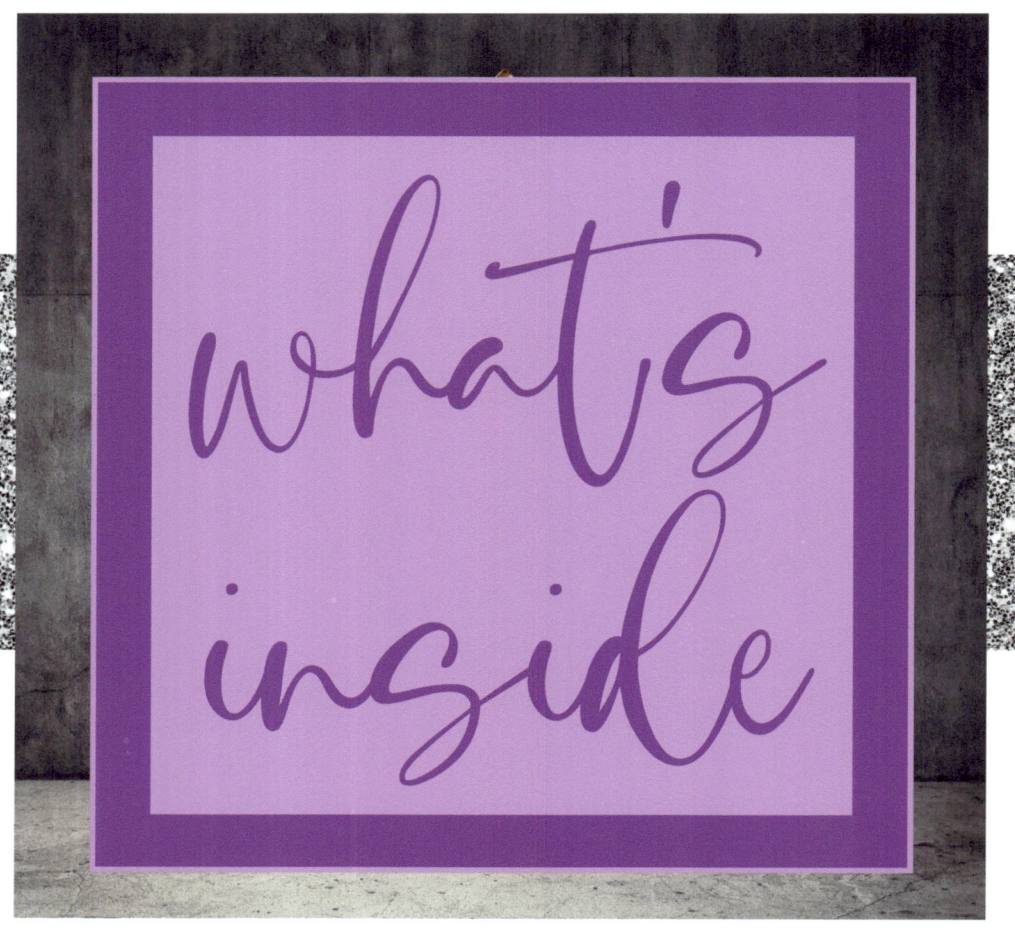

FINANCIAL FREEDOM
is yours

PHILLIPPIANS 4:19

BANK ACCOUNTS

Account name

Bank

_____

Account no _____   Type of account _____

Card no _____   Username _____

Credit limit _____ PIN _____   Password _____

Card type ☐ Credit card ☐ Debit card   Website _____

Account name

Bank

_____

Account no _____   Type of account _____

Card no _____   Username _____

Credit limit _____ PIN _____   Password _____

Card type ☐ Credit card ☐ Debit card   Website _____

Account name

Bank

_____

Account no _____   Type of account _____

Card no _____   Username _____

Credit limit _____ PIN _____   Password _____

Card type ☐ Credit card ☐ Debit card   Website _____

Account name

Bank

_____

Account no _____   Type of account _____

Card no _____   Username _____

Credit limit _____ PIN _____   Password _____

Card type ☐ Credit card ☐ Debit card   Website _____

ACCOUNT TRACKER

ACCOUNT DETAILS

DATE	
BANK	ACCOUNT NO.
STARTING BALANCE	DESCRIPTION
BALANCE	
DEPOSIT	WITHDRAWAL

ACCOUNT DETAILS

DATE	
BANK	ACCOUNT NO.
STARTING BALANCE	DESCRIPTION
BALANCE	
DEPOSIT	WITHDRAWAL

ACCOUNT DETAILS

DATE	
BANK	ACCOUNT NC.
STARTING BALANCE	DESCRIPTION
BALANCE	
DEPOSIT	WITHDRAWAL

MONTHLY BUDGET

MONTH: _____   YEAR: _____

INCOME: _____   INCOME GOAL: _____

INCOME BREAKDOWN		
DATE	DESCRIPTION	AMOUNT

FIXED EXPENSES		
DATE	DESCRIPTION	AMOUNT

VARIABLE EXPENSES		
DATE	DESCRIPTION	AMOUNT

ZERO BUDGET

INCOME	BUDGET	ACTUAL
INCOME TOTAL		

MONTHLY BILLS	DUE	AMOUNT
BILLS TOTAL		
LEFTOVER		

SINKING FUNDS	BUDGET	ACTUAL
SINKING FUNDS TOTAL		
LEFTOVER		

SAVINGS PLAN	BUDGET	ACTUAL
TOTAL SAVINGS		
LEFTOVER		

DEBT PAYMENTS	BUDGET	ACTUAL
TOTAL DEBT		
LEFTOVER		

DAILY LIVING	BUDGET	ACTUAL
DAILY LIVING TOTAL		
FINAL BUDGET (MAKE IT ZERO)		

BUDGET WORKSHEET

MONTH

BUDGET GOAL

SAVINGS GOAL

INCOME

DATE	DESCRIPTION	AMOUNT	AFTER TAX

OTHER EXPENSES

DATE	DESCRIPTION	AMOUNT
TOTAL		

FIXED EXPENSES

DATE	DESCRIPTION	AMOUNT
TOTAL		

SUMMARY

	GOAL	ACTUAL	DIFFERENCE
TOTAL INCOME			
TOTAL EXPENSES			
TOTAL SAVINGS			

CREDIT SCORE TRACKER

Year	Beginning Score	Goal

800 —————————————————————————

600 —————————————————————————

400 —————————————————————————

200 —————————————————————————

0 —————————————————————————

J F M A M J J A S O N D

Q1　　　　Q2　　　　Q3　　　　Q4

January	April	July	October

February	May	August	November

March	June	September	December

SPENDING TRACKER

Weeks	Amount	Total	Weeks	Amount	Total
01			27		
02			28		
03			29		
04			30		
05			31		
06			32		
07			33		
08			34		
09			35		
10			36		
11			37		
12			38		
13			39		
14			40		
15			41		
16			42		
17			43		
18			44		
19			45		
20			46		
21			47		
22			48		
23			49		
24			50		
25			51		
26			52		

Amount Spend: Total Spend:

NO SPEND CHALLENGE

MONTH

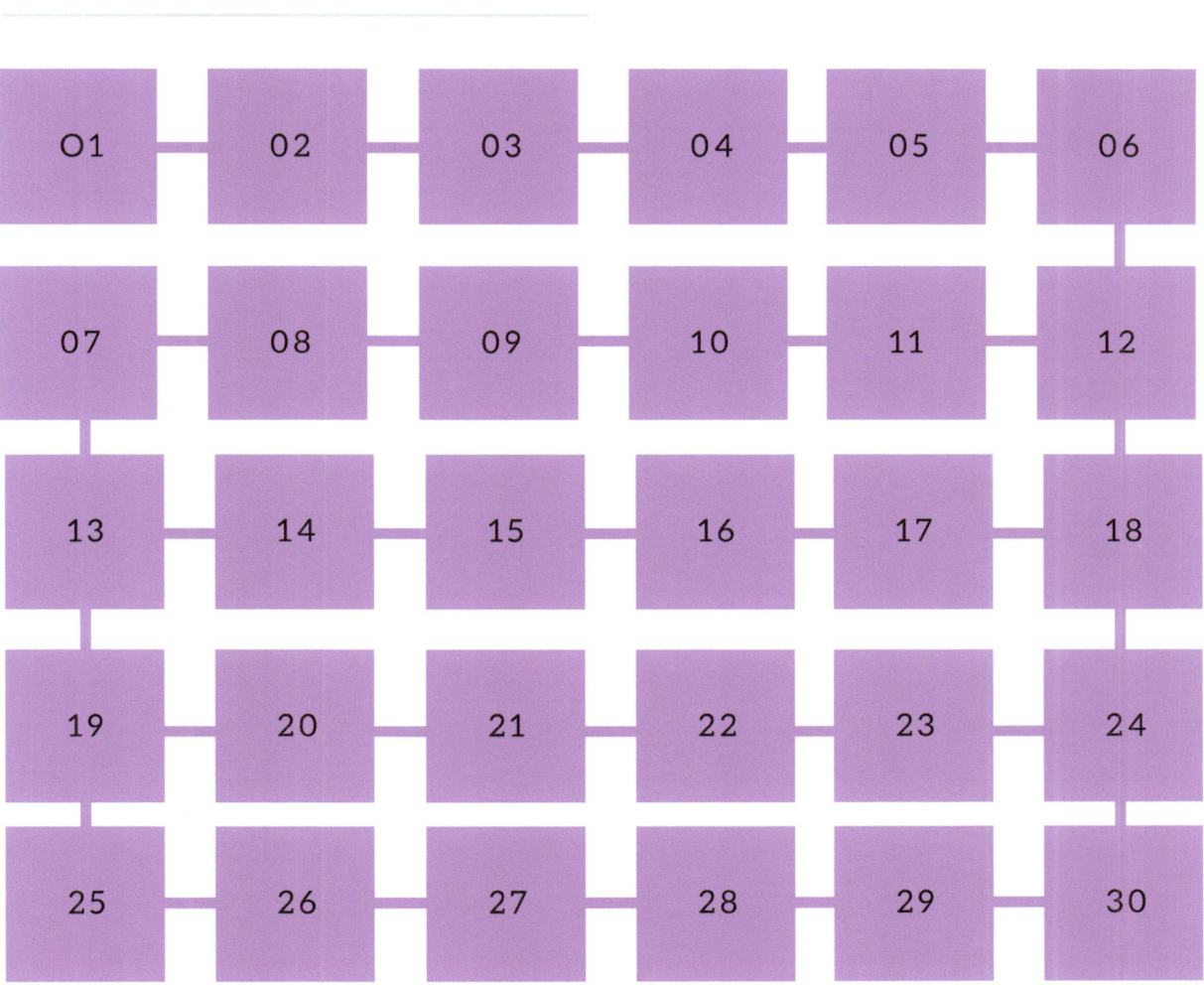

01	02	03	04	05	06
07	08	09	10	11	12
13	14	15	16	17	18
19	20	21	22	23	24
25	26	27	28	29	30

Exceptions

Stats

Reflections

EXPENSES TRACKER

MONTH

DATE	CATEGORY	DESCRIPTION	AMOUNT
		TOTAL:	

PROVERBS 10:22

YEARLY EXPENSES

Year: _____

JANUARY	FEBRUARY	MARCH

APRIL	MAY	JUNE

JULY	AUGUST	SEPTEMBER

OCTOBER	NOVEMBER	DECEMBER

INCOME TRACKER

MONTH

DATE	SOURCE	DESCRIPTION	AMOUNT
		TOTAL:	

BILL TRACKER

BILL	DUE ON	PAID ON	AMOUNT PAID

BILL CHECKLIST

BILLS	DUE	AMOUNT	JAN	FEB	MAR	APR	MAY	JUN	JUL	AUG	SEP	OCT	NOV	DEC

" BUILD WEALTH

DUETORONOMY 8:18

SUBSCRIPTIONS

MONTHLY

SUBSCRIPTION	AMOUNT	JAN	FEB	MAR	APR	MAY	JUN	JUL	AUG	SEP	OCT	NOV	DEC

QUARTERLY

SUBSCRIPTION	AMOUNT	Q1	Q2	Q3	Q4

ONLINE SHOPPING

MONTH   BUDGET

ITEM/S	PRICE	SHOP/WEBSITE	DATE ORDERED	DATE SHIPPED	DATE RECEIVED
			TOTAL:		

SHOPPING LIST

DATE:

Item	Qty	✔

NOTES

BUCKET LIST

DATE:

- [ ]
- [ ]
- [ ]
- [ ]
- [ ]
- [ ]
- [ ]
- [ ]
- [ ]
- [ ]
- [ ]
- [ ]
- [ ]
- [ ]

- [ ]
- [ ]
- [ ]
- [ ]
- [ ]
- [ ]
- [ ]
- [ ]
- [ ]
- [ ]
- [ ]
- [ ]
- [ ]
- [ ]

NOTES

FAMILY BUDGET

1 CHRONICLES 29:12-13

HOUSE EXPENSES	BUDGET	ACTUAL	DIFFERENCE	NOTES

AUTO EXPENSES	BUDGET	ACTUAL	DIFFERENCE	NOTES

INSURANCE EXPENSES	BUDGET	ACTUAL	DIFFERENCE	NOTES

LIVING EXPENSES	BUDGET	ACTUAL	DIFFERENCE	NOTES

MSC EXPENSES	BUDGET	ACTUAL	DIFFERENCE	NOTES

WEEKLY EXPENSES

MONTH: _____   WEEK OF: _____   BUDGET: _____

Monday   DATE: _____

DESCRIPTION	AMOUNT
TOTAL	

Tuesday   DATE: _____

DESCRIPTION	AMOUNT
TOTAL	

Wednesday   DATE: _____

DESCRIPTION	AMOUNT
TOTAL	

Thursday   DATE: _____

DESCRIPTION	AMOUNT
TOTAL	

WEEKLY EXPENSES

MONTH: WEEK OF: BUDGET:

Friday   DATE:

DESCRIPTION	AMOUNT
TOTAL	

Saturday   DATE:

DESCRIPTION	AMOUNT
TOTAL	

Sunday   DATE:

DESCRIPTION	AMOUNT
TOTAL	

Notes:

ANNUAL OVERVIEW

	INCOME	EXPENSES	SAVINGS	END BALANCE
JANUARY				
FEBRUARY				
MARCH				
APRIL				
JUNE				
JULY				
AUGUST				
SEPTEMBER				
OCTOBER				
NOVEMBER				
DECEMBER				
TOTAL				

JEREMIAH 17:7-8

Notes:

UPCOMING EXPENSES

Year: _____

JANUARY	FEBRUARY	MARCH

APRIL	MAY	JUNE

JULY	AUGUST	SEPTEMBER

OCTOBER	NOVEMBER	DECEMBER

FINANCIAL CALENDAR

MONTH OF				YEAR		
MON	TUE	WED	THU	FRI	SAT	SUN

FINANCIAL CALENDAR

MONTH OF			YEAR			
MON	TUE	WED	THU	FRI	SAT	SUN

FINANCIAL CALENDAR

MONTH OF				YEAR		
MON	TUE	WED	THU	FRI	SAT	SUN

FINANCIAL CALENDAR

MONTH OF			YEAR			
MON	TUE	WED	THU	FRI	SAT	SUN

FINANCIAL CALENDAR

MONTH OF			YEAR			
MON	TUE	WED	THU	FRI	SAT	SUN

FINANCIAL CALENDAR

MONTH OF				YEAR		
MON	TUE	WED	THU	FRI	SAT	SUN

FINANCIAL CALENDAR

MONTH OF		YEAR				
MON	TUE	WED	THU	FRI	SAT	SUN

FINANCIAL CALENDAR

MONTH OF				YEAR		
MON	TUE	WED	THU	FRI	SAT	SUN

FINANCIAL CALENDAR

MON	TUE	WED	THU	FRI	SAT	SUN

FINANCIAL CALENDAR

MONTH OF				YEAR		
MON	TUE	WED	THU	FRI	SAT	SUN

FINANCIAL CALENDAR

MON	TUE	WED	THU	FRI	SAT	SUN

FINANCIAL CALENDAR

MONTH OF				YEAR		
MON	TUE	WED	THU	FRI	SAT	SUN

FIXED EXPENSES

JAN FEB MAR APR MAY JUN JUL AUG SEPT OCT NOV DEC

DATE	DESCRIPTION	CATEGORY	AMOUNT PAID

Subtotal:

Total:

VARIABLE EXPENSES

JAN FEB MAR APR MAY JUN JUL AUG SEPT OCT NOV DEC

DATE	DESCRIPTION	CATEGORY	AMOUNT PAID

Subtotal:

Total:

ISAIAH 8:18

PROFIT & LOSS

Month	Revenue	Expenses	Profit	Loss
January				
February				
March				
April				
May				
June				
July				
August				
September				
October				
November				
December				
Yearly Totals				

FINANCE TRACKER

JAN FEB MAR APR MAY JUN JUL AUG SEPT OCT NOV DEC

INCOME	EXPENSES	PROFIT	DESCRIPTION

FINANCIAL SUMMARY

YEAR:

My Income

Jan	Feb	Mar	Apr	May	June	July	Aug	Sep	Oct	Nov	Dec

TOTAL:

My Savings

Jan	Feb	Mar	Apr	May	June	July	Aug	Sep	Oct	Nov	Dec

TOTAL:

My Expenses

Jan	Feb	Mar	Apr	May	June	July	Aug	Sep	Oct	Nov	Dec

TOTAL:

My Credit Cards

Jan	Feb	Mar	Apr	May	June	July	Aug	Sep	Oct	Nov	Dec

TOTAL:

NOTES:

TAX DEDUCTIONS

MONTH

DATE	CATEGORY	EXPENSES	AMOUNT

DONATION TRACKER

DATE	VALUE	DONATED TO	DESCRIPTION

SALES TRACKER

MONTH OF				YEAR		
DATE	ITEM SOLD	ORDER #	SALE PRICE	YOUR COST	FEES	REVENUE

BILLING ACCOUNTS

Bill

COMPANY NAME

CONTACTS

ACCOUNT NO

PAYMENT METHOD

PAYMENT DATE

PAYMENT AMOUNT

ADDRESS

NOTES

Bill

COMPANY NAME

CONTACTS

ACCOUNT NO

PAYMENT METHOD

PAYMENT DATE

PAYMENT AMOUNT

ADDRESS

NOTES

Bill

COMPANY NAME

CONTACTS

ACCOUNT NO

PAYMENT METHOD

PAYMENT DATE

PAYMENT AMOUNT

ADDRESS

NOTES

Bill

COMPANY NAME

CONTACTS

ACCOUNT NO

PAYMENT METHOD

PAYMENT DATE

PAYMENT AMOUNT

ADDRESS

NOTES

Bill

COMPANY NAME

CONTACTS

ACCOUNT NO

PAYMENT METHOD

PAYMENT DATE

PAYMENT AMOUNT

ADDRESS

NOTES

Bill

COMPANY NAME

CONTACTS

ACCOUNT NO

PAYMENT METHOD

PAYMENT DATE

PAYMENT AMOUNT

ADDRESS

NOTES

ONLINE BILLING ACCOUNTS

Bill

COMPANY NAME

CONTACTS

ACCOUNT NO

PAYMENT METHOD

PAYMENT DATE

PAYMENT AMOUNT

ONLINE USERNAME

PASSWORD

NOTES

Bill

COMPANY NAME

CONTACTS

ACCOUNT NO

PAYMENT METHOD

PAYMENT DATE

PAYMENT AMOUNT

ONLINE USERNAME

PASSWORD

NOTES

Bill

COMPANY NAME

CONTACTS

ACCOUNT NO

PAYMENT METHOD

PAYMENT DATE

PAYMENT AMOUNT

ONLINE USERNAME

PASSWORD

NOTES

Bill

COMPANY NAME

CONTACTS

ACCOUNT NO

PAYMENT METHOD

PAYMENT DATE

PAYMENT AMOUNT

ONLINE USERNAME

PASSWORD

NOTES

Bill

COMPANY NAME

CONTACTS

ACCOUNT NO

PAYMENT METHOD

PAYMENT DATE

PAYMENT AMOUNT

ONLINE USERNAME

PASSWORD

NOTES

Bill

COMPANY NAME

CONTACTS

ACCOUNT NO

PAYMENT METHOD

PAYMENT DATE

PAYMENT AMOUNT

ONLINE USERNAME

PASSWORD

NOTES

BILL TRACKER

DATE:

Item Name	Jan	Feb	Mar	Apr	May	June	July	Aug	Sep	Oct	Nov	Dec
TOTAL:												

ANNUAL TOTAL:	

52 WEEKS SAVINGS

DATE

GOAL

	Deposit	End Balance
01		
02		
03		
04		
05		
06		
07		
08		
09		
10		
11		
12		
13		
14		
15		
16		
17		
18		
29		
20		
21		
22		
23		
24		
25		
26		

	Deposit	End Balance
27		
28		
29		
30		
31		
32		
33		
34		
35		
36		
37		
38		
39		
40		
41		
42		
43		
44		
45		
46		
47		
48		
49		
50		
51		
52		

SAVINGS TRACKER

100%

                                                   95%

90%

                                                   85%

80%

                                                   75%

70%

                                                   65%

60%

                                                   55%

50%

                                                   45%

40%

                                                   35%

30%

                                                   25%

20%

                                                   35%

10%

                                                   5%

0%

EMERGENCY FUND

MONTH	ADDED	RUNNING TOTAL

SINKING FUND

MONTH _____   TOTAL _____

FUND NAME	
BEG. BALANCE	
CONTRIBUTIONS	
END. BALANCE	

GOAL AMOUNT

DATE	TRANSACTION	AMOUNT
	TOTAL	

FUND NAME	
BEG. BALANCE	
CONTRIBUTIONS	
END. BALANCE	

GOAL AMOUNT

DATE	TRANSACTION	AMOUNT
	TOTAL	

FUND NAME	
BEG. BALANCE	
CONTRIBUTIONS	
END. BALANCE	

GOAL AMOUNT

DATE	TRANSACTION	AMOUNT
	TOTAL	

FUND NAME	
BEG. BALANCE	
CONTRIBUTIONS	
END. BALANCE	

GOAL AMOUNT

DATE	TRANSACTION	AMOUNT
	TOTAL	

DEBT TRACKER

Creditor _____   Total Debt _____

Start Date		End Date	
ID		Password	
Start Balance		End Balance	
Account No		Interest Rate	

DATE	AMOUNT	BALANCE
TOTAL:		

PAYOFF DEBT

DEBTS					
BALANCE					
PAY / MONTH					
BALANCE					
JAN					
FEB					
MAR					
APR					
MAY					
JUN					
AUG					
SEP					
OCT					
NOV					
DEC					

STEPS TO TAKE

CREDIT CARD PAYOFF

COMPANY	
AMOUNT OWED	
MINIMUM PAYMENT	
INTEREST RATE	
DUE DATE	

DATE	STARTING BALANCE	PAYMENT VALUE	REMAINING BALANCE

FUTURE GOALS

DATE FRAME	WHAT I WANT TO ACHIEVE/VISION	STEPS/ACTIONS
3 Months		
6 Months		
1 Year		
3 Years		
5 Years		

INCOME GOALS

SHORT-TERM GOALS

Goal

Deadline

_____
_____

_____
_____

_____
_____

SHORT-TERM GOALS

Goal

Deadline

_____
_____

_____
_____

_____
_____

SHORT-TERM GOALS

Goal

Deadline

_____
_____

_____
_____

_____
_____

RETIREMENT PLANNING

GOALS		
Goal Retirement Year	Your Age That Year	Goal Net Monthly Income in Retirement

INCOME STREAMS						
Name	Plan Type	Annual Contribution	Start Year	Duration	Estimated Benefit	Taxable

NOTES

RETIREMENT TRACKER

YEAR	CONTRIBUTIONS	BALANCE	NOTES

INVESTMENT TRACKER

DATE	SHARES	ACCOUNT NAME	QTY	FEES

SHARE PERFORMANCE

Company _____   Type _____

Purchased	Qty	Price/Share	Total	Sale Price	Sale Date	Total	Profit/Loss

DIVIDENTS

Date	Amount	Date	Amount	Date	Amount

NOTES

NET WORTH TRACKER

MONTH _____   YEAR _____

TOTAL ASSETS _____   TOTAL LIABILITIES _____

NET WORTH _____

ASSETS		LIABILITIES	
DESCRIPTION	VALUE	DESCRIPTION	VALUE

TO DO LIST

Notes

_____

_____

_____

_____

_____

_____

_____

_____

_____

_____

_____

_____

_____

_____

_____

_____

_____

_____

_____

_____

_____

 # TO DO LIST

DATE : _____

- [ ] _____
- [ ] _____
- [ ] _____
- [ ] _____
- [ ] _____
- [ ] _____
- [ ] _____
- [ ] _____
- [ ] _____
- [ ] _____
- [ ] _____
- [ ] _____

- [ ] _____
- [ ] _____
- [ ] _____
- [ ] _____
- [ ] _____
- [ ] _____
- [ ] _____
- [ ] _____
- [ ] _____
- [ ] _____
- [ ] _____
- [ ] _____

NOTES

PSALMS 112:3

PROVERBS 3:16

PROVERBS 8:21

NOTES

NOTES

NOTES

NOTES

NOTES

NOTES

NOTES

NOTES

NOTES

NOTES

NOTES

DAILY CHECK IN

DATE _____

TODAY I'M GREATFUL FOR
○ _____
○ _____
○ _____

TODAY'S AFFIRMATION

TODAY I FELT

WHAT I WANT TO REMEMBER
ABOUT TODAY

WHAT WAS THE BEST THING
ABOUT TODAY?

THINGS I DID TODAY
○ _____
○ _____
○ _____
○ _____

PEOPLE I MET TODAY

MY RANKING OF TODAY
★ ★ ★ ★ ★

DAILY CHECK IN

DATE _____

TODAY I'M GREATFUL FOR

○ _____
○ _____
○ _____

TODAY'S AFFIRMATION

TODAY I FELT

WHAT I WANT TO REMEMBER ABOUT TODAY

WHAT WAS THE BEST THING ABOUT TODAY?

THINGS I DID TODAY

○ _____
○ _____
○ _____
○ _____

PEOPLE I MET TODAY

MY RANKING OF TODAY

⭐ ⭐ ⭐ ⭐ ⭐

DAILY CHECK IN

DATE _____

TODAY I'M GREATFUL FOR

○ _____
○ _____
○ _____

TODAY'S AFFIRMATION

TODAY I FELT

😀 😊 😐 🙁 ☹️ 😮

WHAT I WANT TO REMEMBER
ABOUT TODAY

WHAT WAS THE BEST THING
ABOUT TODAY?

THINGS I DID TODAY

○ _____
○ _____
○ _____
○ _____

PEOPLE I MET TODAY

MY RANKING OF TODAY

⭐ ⭐ ⭐ ⭐ ⭐

DAILY CHECK IN

DATE _____

TODAY I'M GREATFUL FOR

- ○ _____
- ○ _____
- ○ _____

TODAY'S AFFIRMATION

TODAY I FELT

WHAT I WANT TO REMEMBER ABOUT TODAY

WHAT WAS THE BEST THING ABOUT TODAY?

THINGS I DID TODAY

- ○ _____
- ○ _____
- ○ _____
- ○ _____

PEOPLE I MET TODAY

MY RANKING OF TODAY

★ ★ ★ ★ ★

DAILY CHECK IN

DATE _____

TODAY I'M GREATFUL FOR

○ _____

○ _____

○ _____

TODAY'S AFFIRMATION

TODAY I FELT

😀 🙂 😐 🙁 ☹️ 😮

WHAT I WANT TO REMEMBER
ABOUT TODAY

WHAT WAS THE BEST THING
ABOUT TODAY?

THINGS I DID TODAY

○ _____

○ _____

○ _____

○ _____

PEOPLE I MET TODAY

MY RANKING OF TODAY

⭐ ⭐ ⭐ ⭐ ⭐

DAILY CHECK IN

DATE _____

TODAY I'M GREATFUL FOR
- ○ _____
- ○ _____
- ○ _____

TODAY'S AFFIRMATION

TODAY I FELT

WHAT I WANT TO REMEMBER ABOUT TODAY

WHAT WAS THE BEST THING ABOUT TODAY?

THINGS I DID TODAY
- ○ _____
- ○ _____
- ○ _____
- ○ _____

PEOPLE I MET TODAY

MY RANKING OF TODAY

DAILY CHECK IN

DATE _____

TODAY I'M GREATFUL FOR

○ _____

○ _____

○ _____

TODAY'S AFFIRMATION

WHAT WAS THE BEST THING ABOUT TODAY?

THINGS I DID TODAY

○ _____

○ _____

○ _____

○ _____

TODAY I FELT

PEOPLE I MET TODAY

WHAT I WANT TO REMEMBER ABOUT TODAY

MY RANKING OF TODAY

DAILY CHECK IN

DATE _____

TODAY I'M GREATFUL FOR _____

○ _____

○ _____

○ _____

TODAY'S AFFIRMATION _____

TODAY I FELT _____

😄 🙂 😐 🙁 ☹️ 😲

WHAT I WANT TO REMEMBER
ABOUT TODAY _____

WHAT WAS THE BEST THING
ABOUT TODAY? _____

THINGS I DID TODAY _____

○ _____

○ _____

○ _____

○ _____

PEOPLE I MET TODAY _____

MY RANKING OF TODAY

⭐ ⭐ ⭐ ⭐ ⭐

DAILY CHECK IN

DATE _____

TODAY I'M GREATFUL FOR

○ _____
○ _____
○ _____

TODAY'S AFFIRMATION

TODAY I FELT

WHAT I WANT TO REMEMBER ABOUT TODAY

WHAT WAS THE BEST THING ABOUT TODAY?

THINGS I DID TODAY

○ _____
○ _____
○ _____
○ _____

PEOPLE I MET TODAY

MY RANKING OF TODAY

DAILY CHECK IN

DATE _____

TODAY I'M GREATFUL FOR

○ _____
○ _____
○ _____

TODAY'S AFFIRMATION
_____

WHAT WAS THE BEST THING ABOUT TODAY?

THINGS I DID TODAY

○ _____
○ _____
○ _____
○ _____

TODAY I FELT

PEOPLE I MET TODAY

WHAT I WANT TO REMEMBER ABOUT TODAY

MY RANKING OF TODAY

DAILY CHECK IN

DATE _____

TODAY I'M GREATFUL FOR

○ _____

○ _____

○ _____

TODAY'S AFFIRMATION

TODAY I FELT

😃 🙂 😐 🙁 ☹️ 😮

WHAT I WANT TO REMEMBER ABOUT TODAY

WHAT WAS THE BEST THING ABOUT TODAY?

THINGS I DID TODAY

○ _____

○ _____

○ _____

○ _____

PEOPLE I MET TODAY

MY RANKING OF TODAY

⭐ ⭐ ⭐ ⭐ ⭐

DAILY CHECK IN

DATE _____

TODAY I'M GREATFUL FOR

- ○ _____
- ○ _____
- ○ _____

TODAY'S AFFIRMATION

TODAY I FELT

😀 🙂 😐 😢 ☹️ 😲

WHAT I WANT TO REMEMBER
ABOUT TODAY

WHAT WAS THE BEST THING
ABOUT TODAY?

THINGS I DID TODAY

- ○ _____
- ○ _____
- ○ _____
- ○ _____

PEOPLE I MET TODAY

MY RANKING OF TODAY

⭐ ⭐ ⭐ ⭐ ⭐

DAILY CHECK IN

DATE _____

TODAY I'M GREATFUL FOR

○ _____
○ _____
○ _____

TODAY'S AFFIRMATION

TODAY I FELT

😃 😊 😐 🙁 ☹️ 😮

WHAT I WANT TO REMEMBER ABOUT TODAY

WHAT WAS THE BEST THING ABOUT TODAY?

THINGS I DID TODAY

○ _____
○ _____
○ _____
○ _____

PEOPLE I MET TODAY

MY RANKING OF TODAY

⭐ ⭐ ⭐ ⭐ ⭐

DAILY CHECK IN

DATE _____

TODAY I'M GREATFUL FOR
- ○ _____
- ○ _____
- ○ _____

TODAY'S AFFIRMATION

TODAY I FELT

WHAT I WANT TO REMEMBER ABOUT TODAY

WHAT WAS THE BEST THING ABOUT TODAY?

THINGS I DID TODAY
- ○ _____
- ○ _____
- ○ _____
- ○ _____

PEOPLE I MET TODAY

MY RANKING OF TODAY
★ ★ ★ ★ ★

DAILY CHECK IN

DATE _____

TODAY I'M GREATFUL FOR

○ _____

○ _____

○ _____

TODAY'S AFFIRMATION

TODAY I FELT

WHAT I WANT TO REMEMBER ABOUT TODAY

WHAT WAS THE BEST THING ABOUT TODAY?

THINGS I DID TODAY

○ _____

○ _____

○ _____

○ _____

PEOPLE I MET TODAY

MY RANKING OF TODAY

★ ★ ★ ★ ★

CONNECT WITH **SABRINA ACROSS** SOCIAL MEDIA

www.ingramcontent.com/pod-product-compliance
Lightning Source LLC
Chambersburg PA
CBHW041550120626
46551CB00002B/162